I0053730

Matthias Fiedler

The Concept of Innovative Real Estate Matching: Real Estate Brokerage Made Easy

Real Estate Matching: Efficient, easy and
professional real estate brokerage with an
innovative real estate matching portal

Publishing Details – Impressum | Legal Notice

1.Edition as Print-Book | December 2016
(Originally published in German, December 2016)

© 2016 Matthias Fiedler

Matthias Fiedler
Erika-von-Brockdorff-Str. 19
41352 Korschenbroich
Germany
www.matthiasfiedler.net

Printing and production:
See imprint on last page

Cover Design: Matthias Fiedler
Creation of the E-Book: Matthias Fiedler

ISBN-13 (Paperback): 978-3-00-055319-6
ISBN-13 (E-Book mobi): 978-3-00-055442-1
ISBN-13 (E-Book epub): 978-3-9818618-1-5

Bibliographic information of the Deutsche Nationalbibliothek: The Deutsche Nationalbibliothek records this publication in the Deutsche Nationalbibliografie; detailed bibliographic data are available on the Internet at http://dnb.d-nb.de.

SUMMARY

This book explains a revolutionary concept for a worldwide real estate matching portal (app) with a calculation of the considerable sales potential (Billion Dollar), which is integrated into a real estate agency software including real estate assessment (Trillion Dollar sales potential).

This means that residential and commercial real estate, whether owner-occupied or rented, can be brokered efficiently and in a time-saving manner. It is the future of the innovative and professional real estate brokerage for all real estate agents and property owners. Real estate matching works in almost all countries and even across countries.

Instead of "bringing" properties to the buyer or renter, with a real estate matching portal, potential buyers or renters can be qualified (search profile) and then matched and linked to the properties offered by the real estate agents.

CONTENTS

PREFACE

In 2011 I conceived and developed the idea described here for an innovative real estate matching process.

Since 1998 I have been involved in the real estate business (including real estate brokerage, buying and selling, assessing, rental, and property development). I am a realtor (IHK), real estate economist (ADI) and certified expert in real estate valuation (DEKRA) as well as a member of the internationally recognized real estate association of the Royal Institution of Chartered Surveyors (MRICS).

Matthias Fiedler
Korschenbroich, 10/31/2016
www.matthiasfiedler.net

1. The Concept of Innovative Real Estate Matching: Real Estate Brokerage Made Easy

Real Estate Matching: Efficient, easy and professional real estate brokerage with an innovative real estate matching portal

Instead of "bringing" properties to the buyer or renter, with a real estate matching portal (app), potential buyers or renters can be qualified (search profile) and then matched and linked to the properties offered by the real estate agents.

2. Objectives of Potential Buyers or Renters and Property Vendors

From the perspective of the real estate sellers and landlords, it is important to sell or rent their property quickly and at the highest possible price. From the perspective of the potential buyers and renters, it is important to find the right property to meet their needs and be able to rent it or buy it as quickly and easily as possible.

3. Previous Approaches to Searching Real Estate

Generally, potential real estate buyers or renters use large online real estate portals to look for properties in their preferred region. There, they can have properties or a list of the relevant links to the properties sent to them by e-mail once they have set up a brief search profile. This is frequently done on 2 to 3 real estate portals. Afterward, the vendor is generally contacted by e-mail. As a result, the seller or landlord gets the opportunity and permission to get in touch with the interested party.

In addition, the potential buyers or renters contact individual real estate agents in their region and a search profile is created for them.

The providers on the real estate portals come from both the private and the commercial real estate sector. Commercial providers are predominantly real estate agents and in some cases construction companies, real estate brokers and other real estate companies (in this text, commercial providers are referred to as real estate agents).

4. Disadvantage of Private Providers / Advantage of Real Estate Agents

With real estate properties for sale, private sellers cannot always guarantee an immediate sale. In the case of an inherited property, for example, there may not be a consensus among the heirs or the certificate of inheritance may be missing. In addition, unclear legal issues like the right of residence can complicate the sale.

For rental properties, it can occur that the private landlord has not received the official permits, for example those required to rent a commercial space as a residence.

When a real estate agent is acting as a provider, he has generally already clarified the previously mentioned aspects. Furthermore, all relevant real estate documents (floor plan, site plan, energy certification, title register, official documents, etc.) are usually already available. As a result, the sale or renting can be completed quickly and without complications.

5. Real Estate Matching

In order to match interested buyers or renters with sellers or landlords as quickly and efficiently as possible, it is generally important to take a systematic and professional approach.

This is done here with an approach (or process) that is focused inversely on the searching and finding process between real estate agents and interested parties. This means that instead of "bringing" properties to the buyer or renter, with a real estate matching portal (app), potential buyers or renters can be qualified (search profile) and then matched and linked to the properties offered by the real estate agents.

In the first step, the potential buyers or renters set up a specific search profile in the real estate matching portal. This search profile includes about 20 characteristics. The following characteristics can be included (not a complete listing) and are essential for the search profile.

- Region / Postal Code / City
- Type of object
- Size of property
- Living area
- Purchase price / rent
- Year of construction
- Stories
- Number of rooms
- Rented (yes/no)
- Basement (yes/no)
- Balcony/Terrace (yes/no)
- Method of heating
- Parking space (yes/no)

Important here is that the characteristics are not entered manually but instead are selected by clicking or opening the relevant fields (e.g., type of property) from a list of pre-determined possibilities/options (for type of property: apartment, single family home, warehouse, office, etc.).

If desired, the interested parties can set up additional search profiles. Modifying the search profile is also possible.

In addition, the potential buyers or renters enter complete contact data in the specified fields. These include last name, first name, street, house number, postal code, city, telephone, and e-mail address.

In this context, the interested parties grant their consent to be contacted and to receive matching properties from the real estate agents.

The interested parties hereby also enter into a contract with the operator of the real estate matching portal.

In the next step, the search profiles are made available to the connected real estate agents, not yet visible, via an application programming interface (api) – for example similar to the German programming interface "openimmo". It should be noted here that this programming interface – basically the key for the implementation – should support or guarantee transfer to almost every real estate software solution currently in use. If this is not the case, it should be made technologically possible. Because there are already programming interfaces in use, such as the aforementioned "openimmo", as well as others, it needs to be possible to transfer the search profile.

Now the real estate agents compare the profile with their properties currently on the market. For this purpose, the properties are uploaded to the real estate matching portal and compared and linked to the relevant characteristics.

After the comparison is completed, a report which displays the match in percent is generated. Starting with a 50% match, the search profile is made visible to the real estate agency software.

The individual characteristics are weighted against each other (point system) so that after comparing the characteristics, a percentage for matching (probability of a match) is determined. For example, the characteristic "property type" is weighted higher than the characteristic "living area". In addition, certain characteristics (e.g. basement) can be selected that the property must necessarily have.

In the course of comparing the characteristics for matching, it should also be ensured that the real estate agents only have access to their desired (booked) regions. This reduces the effort for the data comparison. This is particularly important considering real estate agencies frequently operate on a regional basis. It should be noted here that through cloud solutions, it is possible today to store and process large amounts of data.

In order to guarantee professional real estate brokerage, only real estate agents receive access to the search profiles.

To this end, the real estate agents enter into a contract with the operator of the real estate matching portal.

After the relevant comparing/matching, the real estate agent can contact the interested, and conversely the interested parties can contact the real estate agency. If the real estate agent has sent a report to the potential buyer or renter, this also means that an activity report or an agent's claim for the real estate commission is documented in the case of a completed sale or lease.

This is under the condition that the real estate agent is hired by the property owner (seller or landlord) for the placement of the property or that consent has been granted for them to offer the property.

6. Scope of Application

The real estate matching described here is applicable for selling and renting real estate in the residential and commercial sector. For commercial real estate, the respective additional real estate characteristics are required.

There can also be a real estate agent on the side of the potential buyers or renters, as is often done in practice, for instance if he was commissioned by clients.

In terms of geographical regions, the real estate matching portal is applicable in almost every country.

7. Advantages

This real estate matching process offers a big advantage to the potential buyers and sellers, whether they are looking in their own area (place of residence) or are moving to a different city or region for work-related reasons.

They only have to enter their search profile one time to receive information about matching properties from real estate agents operating in the desired region.

For the real estate agents, this provides major advantages in terms of efficiency and time savings for the sale or rental.

They receive an immediate overview of how high the potential for concrete interested parties is regarding each respective property offered by them.

Furthermore, the real estate agents can directly approach their relevant target group, which has given some specific thought to their "dream" property in the process of setting up their search profile. The contact can be established, for instance, by sending out real estate reports.

This increases the quality of the contact with interested parties who know what they are looking for. It also reduces the number of the subsequent property viewing appointments, which in turn reduces the overall marketing period for properties to be brokered.

After the potential buyer or renter has viewed the property to be placed, the purchase contract or lease can be concluded, as in traditional real estate marketing.

8. Sample Calculation (Potential) – only owner-occupied residences and houses (without rental apartments or houses or commercial properties)

The following example will clearly show the potential of the real estate matching portal.

In a geographic area with 250,000 residents, such as the city of Mönchengladbach (Germany), there are - statistically rounded - approximately 125,000 households (2 residents per household). The average rate of relocation is approximately 10%. This means that 12,500 households relocate per year. The proportion of moving in to moving out for Mönchengladbach is not taken into consideration here. Approximately 10,000 households (80%) search for rental properties and about 2,500 households (20%) search for property for sale.

In accordance with the property market report from the advisory committee for the city of Mönchengladbach, there were 2,613 real estate purchases in 2012. This confirms the previously mentioned number of 2,500 potential buyers. There would actually be more, but not every potential buyer was able to find their ideal property. The number of actually interested potential buyers - or, specifically, the number of search profiles - is estimated to be twice as high as the average relocation rate of about 10%, namely 25,000 search profiles. This includes the possibility that the potential buyers have set up multiple search profiles in the real estate matching portal.

It is also worth mentioning that based on experience, about half of all potential buyers and renters so far found their property by working with a real estate agent; adding up to 6,250 households.

Past experience also shows that at least 70% of all households searched for real estate via a real estate portal on the Internet, which is a total of 8,750 households (corresponds to 17,500 search profiles).

If 30% of all potential buyers and sellers, meaning 3,750 households (or 7,500 search profiles) were to set up a search profile with a real estate matching portal (app) for a city like Mönchengladbach, the connected real estate agents could offer suitable properties to potential buyers via 1,500 specific search profiles (20%) and to potential renters via 6,000 specific search profiles (80%).

This means that with an average search duration of 10 months and a sample price of EUR 50 per month for every search profile set up by potential buyers or renters, there is a sales potential of EUR 3,750,000 per year with 7,500 search profiles for a city with 250,000 residents.

Extrapolating this to all of Germany with the population rounded to 80,000,000 (80 million) residents, this results in a sales potential of EUR 1,200,000,000 (EUR 1.2 billion) per year. If 40% of all potential buyers or renters searched for their real estate through the real estate matching portal instead of 30%, the sales potential would increase to EUR 1,600,000,000 (EUR 1.6 billion) per year.

The sales potential refers only to owner-occupied apartments and homes. Rental and investment properties in the residential real estate sector and the total commercial real estate sector are not included in this calculation of potential.

With about 50,000 companies in Germany in the real estate brokerage business (including real estate agencies, construction companies, real estate traders, and other real estate companies), approximately 200,000 employees and a share of 20% of these 50,000 companies using this real estate matching portal with an average of 2 licenses, the result (applying a sample price of EUR 300 per month per license) is a sales potential of EUR 72,000,000 (EUR 72 million) per year. Furthermore, if a regional booking of the local search profiles is implemented, a significant additional sales potential can be generated, depending on the design.

With this enormous potential of possible buyers and renters with specific search profiles, the real estate agents no longer need to update their own database – if they have one – of interested parties. In addition, the number of current search profiles very likely exceeds the number of search profiles created by many real estate agents in their own databases.

If this innovative real estate matching portal were to be used in several countries, potential buyers from Germany could, for example, create a search profile for vacation apartments on the mediterranean island of Majorca (Spain) and the connected real estate agents in Majorca could present their matching apartments to their potential German clients by e-mail. If the reports are in Spanish, potential renters can nowadays simply use a translation program from the Internet to quickly translate the text into German.

In order to be able to implement the matching of search profiles to available properties without language barriers, a comparison of the respective characteristics can be done within the real estate matching portal based on the programmed (mathematical) characteristics, regardless of language, and the relevant language is assigned at the end.

When using the real estate matching portal on all continents, the previously mentioned sales potential (only for those interested in searching) extrapolated very simply would looks as follows.

Global population:
7,500,000,000 (7.5 billion) Residents

1. Population in industrialized countries and largely industrialized countries:
   2,000,000,000 (2.0 billion) Residents

2. Population in emerging countries:
   4,000,000,000 (4.0 billion) Residents

3. Population in developing countries:
   1,500,000,000 (1.5 billion) Residents

The annual sales potential for Germany is converted and projected as EUR 1.2 billion with 80 million residents with the following assumed factors for industrialized, emerging, and developing countries.

1. Industrialized countries: 1.0

2. Emerging countries: 0.4

3. Developing countries: 0.1

The result is the following annual sales potential (EUR 1.2 billion x population (industrialized, emerging, or developing countries) / 80 million residents x factor).

1. Industrialized
   countries: EUR   30.00 billion
2. Emerging
   countries: EUR   24.00 billion
3. Developing
   countries: EUR   2.25 billion

Total: **EUR**   **56.25 billion**

9. Conclusion

The illustrated real estate matching portal offers significant advantages for those searching for real estate (interested parties) and for real estate agents.

1. The time needed to search for suitable properties is significantly reduced for interested parties because they only need to create their search profile one time.

2. The real estate agent gets an overall view of the number of potential buyers or renters, including information on their specific needs (search profile).

3. The interested parties receive only the desired or matching properties (based on the search profile) from all real estate agents (much like an automatic pre-selection).

4. The real estate agents reduce their effort to maintain their own database of search

profiles because numerous current search profiles are permanently available.

5. Since only commercial providers/real estate agents are connected to the real estate matching portal, the potential buyers or renters can work with experienced real estate agents.

6. The real estate agents reduce their number of viewing appointments and the overall marketing period. In return, the number of viewing appointments for potential buyers or renters is reduced as well as the time for a concluded purchase contract or lease.

7. The owners of the properties to be sold or rented save time as well. There are furthermore financial benefits, with less vacant time for rental properties and sooner purchase payment for properties for sale as the result of a quicker rental or sale.

By implementing this concept in real estate matching, significant progress can be achieved in real estate brokerage.

10. Integrating the Real Estate Matching Portal into New Real Estate Agency Software, Including Real Estate Assessment

As a final comment, the real estate matching portal described here can be a significant component of a new - ideally globally available - real estate agency software solution from the very beginning. This means that the real estate agents can either use the real estate matching portal in addition to their existing real estate agency software solutions, or ideally use the new real estate agency software solution including the real estate matching portal.

By integrating this efficient and innovative real estate matching portal into a new real estate agency software, a fundamental unique selling point for the real estate agency software is created that will be essential for market penetration.

Since real estate assessment is and will remain an essential component of the real estate agency, the real estate agency software must feature an integrated real estate assessment tool. The real estate assessment with the corresponding calculation methods can access the relevant data parameters from the real estate agency's entered/saved properties. Likewise, the real estate agent can make up for missing parameters with his own regional market expertise.

Furthermore, the real estate agency software should have the option of integrating virtual real estate tours of available properties. This could be easily implemented by developing an additional app for mobile phones and/or tablets that can record and then integrate or incorporate the virtual real estate tour - largely automatically - into the real estate agency software.

If the efficient and innovative real estate matching portal is incorporated into a new real estate agency software together with real estate appraisal, the possible sales potential is again increased significantly.

Matthias Fiedler

Korschenbroich, 10/31/2016

Matthias Fiedler

Erika-von-Brockdorff-Str. 19

41352 Korschenbroich

Germany

www.matthiasfiedler.net

www.ingramcontent.com/pod-product-compliance
Lightning Source LLC
Chambersburg PA
CBHW071530210326
41597CB00018B/2948